T 9088

WITHDRAWN

	DATE DUE		

Sarah Childress Polk

Sarah Childress Polk

1803–1891

BY SUSAN SINNOTT

CHILDREN'S PRESS®
A Division of Grolier Publishing
New York   London   Hong Kong   Sydney
Danbury, Connecticut

Consultants	JAYNE CRUMPLER DeFIORE, PH.D.
	Department of Independent Study
	University of Tennessee, Knoxville
	LINDA CORNWELL
	Learning Resource Consultant
	Indiana Department of Education

Project Editor: DOWNING PUBLISHING SERVICES
Page Layout: CAROLE DESNOES
Photo Researcher: JAN IZZO

Visit Children's Press on the Internet at:
http://publishing.grolier.com

Library of Congress Cataloging-in-Publication Data
Sinnott, Susan
    Sarah Childress Polk / by Susan Sinnott.
      p. cm. — (Encyclopedia of first ladies)
    Includes bibliographical references and index.
    Summary: A biography of the First Lady who served as personal secretary to her husband,
the eleventh president of the United States, and who was thereby involved in the daily
workings of his administration.
    ISBN 0-516-20601-X
    1. Polk, Sarah Childress, 1803–1891—Juvenile literature. 2. Presidents' spouses—
United States—Biography—Juvenile literature. 3. Polk, James K. (James Knox),
1795–1849—Juvenile literature. 4. United States—Politics and government—1845–1849—
Juvenile literature. [1. Polk, Sarah Childress, 1803–1891. 2. First ladies. 3. Women—
Biography. 4. Polk, James K. (James Knox), 1795–1849.]
    I. Title. II. Series.
E417.1.S56   1998   98-21381
973.6'1'092—dc21   CIP
[B]   AC

18148

Table of Contents

Sarah Childress Polk

CHAPTER ONE

"A Great Deal of Spice"

☆ ☆ ☆ ☆ ☆ ☆ ☆ ☆ ☆ ☆ ☆ ☆ ☆ ☆ ☆ ☆

Public receptions at the White House had become a beloved tradition. Sarah Polk seemed to enjoy them tremendously. The doors were opened early on Tuesday and Friday evenings, and the public—senators, foreign ministers, merchants, farmers, judges, and shopkeepers—filed in. President Polk, never known for his warmth or charm, was not the main attraction at these events. It seemed as though visitors were rushed past him as fast as they could be introduced. An attendant bellowed, "Gentleman-who-have-been-presented-will-please-walk-into-the-East-Room-don't-block-up-the-passage!" Another attendant looked

☆ ☆ ☆ ☆ ☆ ☆ ☆ ☆ ☆ ☆ ☆ ☆ ☆ ☆ ☆ ☆

Fashion Statements

* * * * * * * * * * * * * * * *

By the time Sarah Polk was wearing the elegant dresses of a first lady, full, floor-length skirts were very much the fashion. Women began to wear hoops, which were stiff undergarments that held their skirts out. Their dresses were trimmed with fancy ruffles, puffs, and lace. Shirring—fabric that was gathered until it puckered—decorated bodices and sleeves. Plaids and checks were popular, perhaps because many Scottish and Irish immigrants had come to the United States. Of course, no self-respecting woman left her home without a bonnet. Several recent inventions made clothing fit better and dressmaking easier. Elastic, hooks and eyes for fastening, machine-made lace, the tape measure, and paper dress patterns were changing the way people made clothing. In 1846, Elias Howe invented the automatic sewing machine. Now clothing could be made faster than ever.

Sarah Polk wore this gown during her husband's administration.

10

ready to nudge anyone who didn't move fast enough. There would be a quick presidential handshake, a word or two, and then on to the East Room.

Visitors were no doubt relieved to walk the few steps to meet the First Lady. Sarah Polk, elegantly dressed in a deep blue or purple velvet gown, with perhaps a tassel in her hair, sat on a plush sofa and graciously held out her hand. She seemed intent on making everyone feel welcome. If someone were to ask the First Lady a policy question—and many did—her eyes would light up and she would give her opinion enthusiastically. No wonder one admirer had written that Mrs. Polk ". . . looked as if she had a great deal of spice!"

Sarah couldn't be considered a great beauty, but her dark looks gave her an air of elegance and exoticism. Many said she looked more like a member of Spanish nobility—some called her jokingly "Madonna"—than the daughter of a Tennessee planter. A devout Presbyterian all her life, she cared little for material things, except perhaps the gowns she wore so ele-

gantly. As was the fashion of the day, she wore her black hair gathered behind her head, with long ringlets framing either side of her face.

As striking as many found her appearance, it was her warmth, wit, and intellectual curiosity that were admired by statesmen and ordinary citizens alike. Sarah read widely, studying the important issues of the day in order to bring varied points of view to her husband's attention. The president relied greatly on her judgment and once confessed that he trusted her more than anyone else.

Yet as close as President and Mrs. Polk were, their personal styles were very different. President Polk was a cold and distant man. Sarah was warm and expansive. James Polk was wise enough to know he needed Sarah's lighter touch. He made her his personal secretary, and she thus became the first First Lady to be brought into the daily workings of her husband's administration. The president was a great proponent of the doctrine of Manifest Destiny—that it was preordained that America's borders should reach from sea to sea. Sarah's work as

Home Improvement

⋆ ⋆

Nine presidential families lived in the White House before the Polks. Each made their own improvements to the mansion. Popular presidents received funds from Congress to buy furnishings and decorate rooms. Andrew Jackson received $50,000 to improve the interior. He spent much of that sum on the elegant East Room, indoor plumbing, and chinaware. Some presidents had to raise their own funds for household needs. The unpopular President Tyler received no money to improve the home. Therefore, when Sarah and James moved in, the White House needed attention. The Polks didn't seem to mind, however. They began a series of interior improvements that included adding gas lighting to the mansion.

This china bowl and the dinner plate at the right were part of the White House china during the Polk administration.

12

The term Manifest Destiny was coined in the 1840s. It expressed the popular belief that the United States had a right to spread across the entire continent. The population was growing fast, and Americans felt the need to expand. They believed it was their right—in the name of democracy—to conquer the land and the native peoples who already lived there. Some expansionists even hoped to bring British North America (now Canada) and all of Mexico under the American flag. President Polk strongly believed in Manifest Destiny. During his presidency, he nearly doubled the size of the United States by adding land in the Southwest and the Northwest. By the end of his term, the United States had assumed most of its modern borders. Expansionist fever died down after 1848. In later years, however, the United States went on to add Alaska and Hawaii, as well as Puerto Rico and islands in the Pacific.

personal secretary kept her focused on the small details of the presidency.

Despite her ambition and strong opinions—unusual for a politician's wife in the 1840s—Sarah's personal charm always seemed to carry the day. Once, sitting on a sofa in the White House East Room, a gentleman from South Carolina came in to greet the First Lady. His voice boomed above the rest of the visitors: "Madame, I have long wished to see the lady upon whom the Bible pronounces a woe!" The others stood in stunned silence, nervously awaiting what would come next. Sarah merely turned to the gentleman calmly, waiting for him to continue. "Does not the Bible say, 'Woe unto you when all men speak well of you!'? . . . and that is certainly the case with you, Madame!" Sarah laughed graciously and the party continued.

CHAPTER TWO

Nothing but the Best

★ ★ ★ ★ ★ ★ ★ ★ ★ ★ ★ ★ ★ ★ ★ ★ ★

Joel Childress was in many ways a classic American success story. Of Scotch-Irish descent, he was born in Campbell County, Virginia, in 1769. In the 1790s, he moved to Sumner County, Tennessee. He grew up in a grating frontier poverty that, had he been a less ambitious, determined man, would have been the whole of his life's story. From the moment Joel Childress cut down his first tree, however, he was set on a path that would take him out of poverty and into comfortable wealth. When he moved to Murfreesboro just before the nineteenth century began, he was already a wealthy planter, landowner, and merchant.

★ ★ ★ ★ ★ ★ ★ ★ ★ ★ ★ ★ ★ ★ ★ ★ ★

Sarah's mother, Elizabeth Whitsitt Childress

He bought a tavern and store on the town square, near the courthouse, and became well acquainted with Tennessee's leading men.

By the time Sarah Childress was born on September 4, 1803, Joel and his wife, Elizabeth Whitsitt Childress, had moved to a plantation just outside Murfreesboro. They had two other children, Anderson and Susan. Not long afterward, Elizabeth Childress gave birth to another son, John. The family lived happily in a magnificently furnished home. The children, too, were given the best Mr. Childress could afford. They dressed in silks and satins and never knew, as Sarah remembered, "what it was to be simply clothed."

Fortunately for the children, "the best" extended to education—for the daughters as well as the sons. This was certainly unusual. At the time, especially in Tennessee, the notion of educating girls past primary school was nothing short of radical. Joel Childress, however, was determined to have his daughters go to the best schools he could find for them. When Sarah and Susan finished the local public school, Mr. Childress petitioned the trustees of Bradley Academy to admit his daughters. Bradley, the school Anderson Childress attended, was a boys' school in Murfreesboro. The school agreed to let the girls receive private instruc-

Profile of America, 1803: Thinking Big

★ ★

The young United States was really thinking big in 1803, the year of Sarah Childress's birth. The population was growing fast. There were more than 5.25 million Americans by then, and many of them were children. People were proud of their new country and eager to expand it. They moved farther and farther west, pushing the boundary of civilization to the Mississippi River. Travel wasn't easy. Before railroads, canals or good roads, it took six weeks to journey from the East Coast to the Mississippi River. Pioneers followed rivers and wagon trails, and crossed the mountains through "gaps," or passes. They settled in such places as the Ohio Valley, where they found rich farmland. In 1803, Ohio became the seventeenth state to join the Union.

A ford on the Cumberland River

The urge to grow affected even the highest office in the land. In the largest real-estate deal in history, President Thomas Jefferson bought 505 million acres (204 hectares) of land from the French in 1803. Stretching from the Mississippi River to the Rocky Mountains, and from the Gulf of Mexico to Canada, this "Louisiana Purchase" doubled the size of the United States. It cost the country $15 million. Americans applauded the purchase, and the most popular song in 1803 became one called "Jefferson and Liberty."

No one knew who or what occupied this vast territory, so in 1804 the president sent William Clark and Meriwether Lewis to explore it. They studied animals, plants, weather, and the landscape to give Jefferson a picture of the new lands. Lewis and Clark returned in 1806 with wonderful reports of the rugged West. And what of the Native Americans who lived there? Lewis and Clark were instructed to assure them of "our wish to be neighborly, friendly, and useful to them."

The Polk family home in Columbia, Tennessee

tion on the campus each afternoon, after the boys' classes had ended.

One day as Sarah, Susan, and Mrs. Childress arrived at Bradley Academy for the two hours of instruction, they were surprised to find Anderson Childress waiting for them. The reason? He wanted to introduce them to his new friend and classmate, James Polk. James, originally from North Carolina, now lived in nearby Columbia. Mrs. Childress invited James to their home for dinner. Sarah remembered much later that the whole family found him very likable. At the time, she was only eleven. James was nineteen.

Anderson Childress and James Polk graduated from Bradley Academy in 1815. James, who was first in the

*The University of North Carolina at Chapel Hill
as it looked about 1827*

senior class, headed off to the University of North Carolina in Chapel Hill. Sarah and Susan finished their studies at Bradley Academy, too. The next fall, they moved in with family friends in Nashville. There, they would attend Mr. Abercrombie's School for Young Ladies. When, at fourteen, Sarah completed that school's program, her father looked around for a school of higher education for his daughters.

Joel Childress finally decided to send Sarah and Susan to the Moravian Female Academy in Salem, North Carolina (today Salem College in Winston-Salem, North Carolina). The academy had been founded in

19

The Moravian Brethren

* *

This religious group was founded in Moravia, today a part of the Czech Republic. However, it gained most of its support in Germany after 1722. The Moravians based their beliefs solely on Bible teachings and believed in spreading Christianity around the world. They came to America in 1735 as missionaries and founded the town of Bethlehem, Pennsylvania. That is still the center of the Moravian church in the United States. The Moravians opened the first school west of the Allegheny Mountains and established the academy in Salem, North Carolina, where Sarah Childress attended school. Moravian colonists laid out Salem, whose name means "peace," in 1766. To this day, a Moravian Easter sunrise service is held there each year. There are about 55,000 Moravians in America today.

Sarah and Susan Childress attended the Moravian Academy in Salem, North Carolina. Today, it is Salem College in the town of Winston-Salem.

1772 by members of the Moravian sect, which had already established highly respected boarding schools in Germany, England, and the United States. The Moravian Female Academy drew students from all over the East Coast. Yet newspaper editors in Tennessee harped against sending girls to fancy schools. Why spend so much time and money, their arguments went, teaching girls European ways and making them "unfitted for the society in which they move?"

Sarah Childress was thrilled to have the chance to break away from the closed world of Middle Tennessee. On a June morning in 1817, fourteen-year-old Sarah and her sister, Susan, set off on horseback. Escorted by Anderson Childress and a male slave, they rode the 200 miles (322 kilometers) across the Great Smoky Mountains to Salem. Once there, the girls put on close-fitting white lace caps—the only required part of their clothing—and began to study under the Moravian brethren.

The Moravians emphasized simple living, thorough teaching, and disciplined thinking. Sarah studied history,

In this painting, Sarah's sister Susan Childress is wearing the type of close-fitting lace cap worn by girls at the Moravian Academy.

literature, and geography, as well as music and drawing. (She tried to get out of needlepoint and housekeeping; the domestic arts would never be Sarah's strong point.) She was encouraged to read widely, and she developed a lifelong love of books.

Joel Childress gave Sarah a tremendous gift by seeing that she was

The Great Smoky Mountains

★ ★

These mountains are part of the larger range called the Appalachian Mountains. The Appalachians run from Canada all the way into Georgia and Alabama. At first, the Cherokee people lived here. They hunted, fished, and gathered wild foods in the lush forests. They called the mountains the "blue smoke place" because the Great Smokies are almost always covered with a blue haze. Settlers cut wood from the mountain forests to build homes and barns. Later, timber companies cut down millions of trees. To save the beauty of the region, the Great Smoky Mountains National Park was formed in 1934. Today, it is home to more than 60 species of mammals and more than 200 kinds of birds.

well educated. In the spring of 1819, Mr. Childress became critically ill and the girls were forced to return to Tennessee. Yet even the one year at the Female Academy marked Sarah's character for the rest of her life.

Sarah was inconsolable as she rode back to Murfreesboro to be at her father's side. She knew there was little hope of his recovering. She also knew that after his death, she and Susan would need to remain home with their mother. Sarah couldn't help but remember how, just the spring before, she'd felt so confident about the future. Now, as she returned to tiny Murfreesboro and her grieving mother, Sarah couldn't help but wonder when, if ever, she'd journey into the wide world again.

★ ★ ★ ★ ★ ★ ★ ★ ★ ★ ★ ★ ★ ★ ★

CHAPTER THREE

James and Sarah

★ ★ ★ ★ ★ ★ ★ ★ ★ ★ ★ ★ ★ ★ ★

Sarah found some consolation in the fact that tiny Murfreesboro had become something of a boom-town. Why, it was even making a pitch to become the state capital of Tennessee! A few ambitious citizens had raised the money to enlarge the small courthouse on the town square. When the renovations were complete, they convinced the state legislature to hold its first meeting there. (The governor's office remained in Nashville, where the legislature moved, too, in 1825.)

The activity of the legislators, clerks, lawyers, and their staffs—many of them eligible young men—gave the small town an exciting bustle. Sarah Childress

★ ★ ★ ★ ★ ★ ★ ★ ★ ★ ★ ★ ★ ★ ★

Tennessee governor William Carroll

for Governor William Carroll. There, she was reintroduced to Mr. Polk. The two were quickly taken with each other. James couldn't help but admire the cultured, sophisticated young woman Sarah had become. Sarah thought that James had an air of achievement and ambition. He had graduated from the University of North Carolina and had studied law.

James Polk was chief clerk of the state senate when Sarah was reintroduced to him in 1822.

became particularly interested in the young lawyer who had recently been elected chief clerk of the state senate. He was said to be a rising star among the Democrats. She'd met him once before: He was Anderson's former school friend, James K. Polk.

One evening in 1822, Sarah attended a reception in Murfreesboro

Andrew Jackson (1767–1845)

✫ ✫

A hero of the War of 1812 and a renowned Indian fighter, Andrew Jackson was a new kind of political figure. "Old Hickory"—so-called because he was as tough as hickory, a very hard wood—was born on the frontier and had the manners and dress of the common folk. Ordinary Americans loved him, but his rough ways and belief in the rights of individuals made him many enemies in Washington. Jackson served two terms as president between 1829 and 1837. Out of his loyal following of frontiersmen, farmers, and workers grew the Democratic party. He was a friend and supporter of James Polk, with whom he shared a desire to expand the nation. Polk was often referred to as "Young Hickory" by young Democrats who hoped he would follow in Jackson's footsteps.

He had been admitted to the Tennessee bar and elected clerk of the state senate.

The position of clerk was very respectable, even though the salary was only $6.00 a day. As clerk, James needed to keep track of bills, reports, resolutions, and other papers. He helped move legislation from floor to committee, back to the floor, from senate to house, and eventually to the governor for final approval. Despite the poor pay, the job gave James a very close look at what would become his life's work. It confirmed for him that politics was more than an interest; it was also a passion.

James and Sarah saw each other as

often as James's duties allowed. Sarah seemed to understand and encourage James's ever-increasing political ambition, even if it took him away from her. Hard-working James, however, may not have understood that a balance between one's political and personal life was necessary, too. So his

friend General Andrew Jackson, who would become the seventh president in 1829, set him straight. Early in 1823, James asked his distinguished friend how he could succeed in politics. General Jackson replied that James should stop dallying about and get married. James mentioned that he thought he'd found a suitable mate in Sarah Childress. Jackson, who was acquainted with the Childress family, gave his very enthusiastic support to the choice.

To be sure, James didn't quite match Sarah in good looks or wealth—despite the fact that his father, Samuel Polk, was himself a prosperous Tennessee planter. Nor were his church-going habits all Sarah or Mrs. Childress might

James Polk, candidate for the Tennessee House of Representatives, rode on horseback as he campaigned throughout his rural district.

28

In September 1823, Representative James Polk attended his first legislative session at the Murfreesboro courthouse, shown here as it looked in 1857.

have wanted. James rarely went to church. Sarah knew, however, that they had many things in common: intelligence, ambition, and a deep belief in themselves.

Sarah accepted James's proposal with one condition: the wedding date would not be set until James improved his financial standing. A clerk's salary was simply too low to support a married couple. James was surprised at such a request, but soon agreed. In 1822, he entered his name as a candidate for Tennessee's House of Representatives.

The campaign was grueling as Candidate Polk spent the summer of 1823 riding on horseback throughout his rural district. He tried to convince country squires and small farmers alike that he understood their needs. James felt he had to shake hands with every voter and risked his health—not for the last time—trying. Meanwhile, Sarah and her mother began the wedding preparations. Fortunately for the young couple, James Polk was elected to the Tennessee House in August 1823. The wedding date was set soon after—New Year's Day, 1824.

David Crockett (1786–1836)

✶ ✶

Colorful frontiersman "Davy" Crockett was born in Tennessee. He served as an Indian scout under Andrew Jackson. After three terms in Congress, Crockett broke with the president because he opposed the policy of moving the Indians off their land. He lost his seat in 1835. Crockett had a gift for telling tall tales. He wrote three books about his life and adventures that made him a living legend and "king of the wild frontier." He died at the Alamo in 1836 fighting for Texas's independence from Mexico.

Representative Polk attended his first legislative session at the end of September. It was, to say the least, a varied group that gathered to make laws for the state of Tennessee. Filing into Murfreesboro's old courthouse were elegantly dressed lawyers from Nashville, weather-beaten small farmers from East Tennessee, newly rich planters from the cotton counties, and of course, politically ambitious young men from all over the state. The most memorable representative, however, was surely the man from the state's

Colonel Davy Crockett, former frontiersman, was the most famous representative of the 1823 Tennessee state legislature.

new western district—the famous frontiersman, Colonel Davy Crockett.

Meanwhile, it seemed that all of Middle Tennessee had set aside New Year's week to attend one of the many wedding parties for James and Sarah. The wedding itself took place on a Thursday evening at the Childress plantation. The marriage service followed a sumptuous seven-course dinner. Parties continued until Tuesday, when the new Mr. and Mrs. Polk traveled to Columbia, 30 miles (48 km) southwest of Murfreesboro, to be hon-

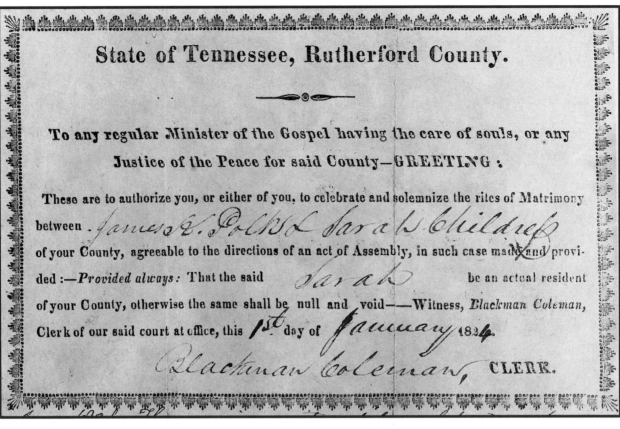

The marriage license of James K. Polk and Sarah Childress

ored by the Polk family and their friends. This was Sarah's first introduction to the entire Polk clan. Most of them—as was the custom—had not attended the festivities near Murfreesboro. Instead, they waited for the couple to come to their own homes.

What did the Polk family think of the new Mrs. James K. Polk? They liked her immediately. Sarah, as always, was at her best in a social situation and succeeded in putting the entire family at ease. She had her opinions, and never hesitated to

Tennessee, U.S.A.

☆ ☆ ☆ ☆ ☆ ☆ ☆ ☆ ☆ ☆ ☆ ☆ ☆ ☆ ☆ ☆ ☆ ☆ ☆ ☆

The people who settled Tennessee knew what they wanted: complete and independent self-government. Pioneers who lived there in 1772 were too far away to care much for the British colonial governor, so they formed their own government. This was the first American attempt at complete independence. The settlers elected officials to make and uphold the law. After the United States gained independence from Britain, North Carolina claimed the lands of Tennessee. But determined Tennesseans formed a state they called "Frankland," or land of the free. It was later changed to "Franklin" for the great patriot Benjamin Franklin. Franklin never really materialized, but less than a decade later, Tennessee joined the Union as the sixteenth state.

advance them, but she was always polite and gracious.

Sarah was understandably relieved when she and James finally arrived at their new home, a two-room cottage James had rented for one year. Other well-to-do brides might have looked at the tiny place and wept, but Sarah adored it. Its size was perfect for her since it required her to do almost no housework. With few domestic chores, she could accompany James to the state capitol each day—which was exactly what she intended to do!

☆ ☆ ☆ ☆ ☆ ☆ ☆ ☆ ☆ ☆ ☆ ☆ ☆ ☆ ☆

CHAPTER FOUR

The Polks Go to Washington

☆ ☆ ☆ ☆ ☆ ☆ ☆ ☆ ☆ ☆ ☆ ☆ ☆ ☆ ☆

James and Sarah Polk were considered a handsome couple indeed as they began their life together. She was only twenty, bright and elegant; he was twenty-eight and fiercely devoted to his career. James Polk, everyone in Murfreesboro believed, was a man with a big future. At the end of the 1823 legislative session, his Uncle Lucius wrote to relatives in North Carolina, "James is one of the first young men in the state." He further predicted that James would soon be elected to the U.S. Congress.

James Polk's political fortunes indeed rose very quickly. With the support of Andrew Jackson, who was

☆ ☆ ☆ ☆ ☆ ☆ ☆ ☆ ☆ ☆ ☆ ☆ ☆ ☆ ☆

Sarah grew very close to her mother-in-law, Jane Knox Polk (above).

left the University of North Carolina! In that short time, he had become one of Tennessee's most prominent lawyers and legislators and now he was going to Washington City. What's more, it looked quite possible that their good friend Mr. Jackson would one day occupy the White House. Who knew what that would mean for a fellow Tennessean and loyal Democrat?

Sarah Polk's joy at her husband's achievements was tempered by his many absences from the little house they rented. Still, she had plenty of company among the ever-growing Polk family, which included the families of James's brothers and sisters. Sarah grew very close to her mother-in-law, Jane Polk, with whom she shared a deep religious devotion. Sarah also often made the 60-mile (97-km) trip back and forth to visit her own mother near Murfreesboro.

In the fall of 1825, Congressman-elect James K. Polk left Sarah at their cottage and set off on horseback for the nation's capital. Accompanied by other members of the Tennessee delegation, he rode across Kentucky and through the Appalachian Mountains.

narrowly defeated in his bid for the presidency in 1824, James Polk entered the race for one of Tennessee's congressional seats. His candidacy was a long shot, but—ever the determined and tireless campaigner—James won by a narrow margin in August 1825.

Sarah was very proud of her husband's stunning success. To think it had been just seven years since he'd

36

Getting There Is Half the Fun

☆ ☆

The first road system in the United States took shape in the late eighteenth century. At that time, stagecoaches required roads that would be passable in all kinds of weather. Until then, most roads were little more than muddy ruts strewn with tree stumps, holes, and rocks. Many roads in the eastern United States were toll roads. "Corduroy roads" were surfaced with tree trunks laid across the width of the road. Plank roads were lined with split logs. Local communities did not have the money to keep up with the demand for roads. In 1806, Congress authorized the construction of the National Road. It ran from Cumberland, Maryland, to Vandalia, Illinois. Sometimes referred to as the Cumberland Road, this highway opened up travel to the West.

Route of the National Road

Finally, in southern Ohio, they reached the National Road. This was a relatively straight route that took them to Baltimore. From there, the men boarded a stagecoach bound for Washington.

Many congressmen, including those with families, lived alone in Washington. They often rented rooms in boardinghouses. James, along with several other Tennesseans, moved into such a house on Capitol Hill. Though

37

In the fall of 1825, when James and the other members of the Tennessee delegation reached Baltimore, they boarded a stagecoach bound for Washington.

each man had his own room, all took meals together at a long table in the dining room.

Sarah wrote often from Tennessee. One of her letters began, "Nothing to communicate," and then included a full account of local goings-on, including analyses of issues of importance to the congressional district. Before closing, Sarah always added a stern

Before the members of the Tennessee delegation reached Baltimore on the way to Washington, they had to cross the Appalachian Mountains (opposite) on horseback.

warning to James to take care of his health, which she knew could be very fragile. "Let me beg and pray," she concluded one of her letters, "that you will take care of yourself and do not become too much excited."

James didn't return to Tennessee for more than six months. Sarah found the long, gray winter very difficult without him. By this time, she had become resigned to the fact that they wouldn't have children. Sarah's deep faith must have allowed her to accept childlessness without bitterness; in

During their trip to Washington in 1826, Sarah and James traveled in a stagecoach through the Blue Ridge Mountains of Virginia.

any case, she never spoke of regret in her letters. She did, however, become determined to join James in Washington and experience that city's excitement firsthand.

Sarah and James returned to Washington together in November 1826. They traveled comfortably in their own stagecoach. The route took them through eastern Tennessee and into western Virginia (now West Virginia), and through the Blue Ridge

Samuel Houston (1793–1863)

✶ ✶

A great friend of Andrew Jackson and Davy Crockett, Sam Houston also grew up on the frontier. Having served in Jackson's army and in the U.S. House of Representatives, Houston was elected governor of Tennessee in 1827. After his wife left him in 1829, he resigned the post and ended up in Texas, which was then under the rule of the Mexican government. Houston took up the cause of independence from Mexico and led Texans into battle when the fighting started. He defeated the Mexican army at San Jacinto and captured Mexican general Santa Anna. In exchange for his freedom, Santa Anna gave Texas its independence. Houston was elected president of the Republic of Texas and worked for its annexation to the United States, which came in 1845.

Mountains of Virginia. They were joined for part of the way by a fellow Tennessee congressman, the flamboyant Sam Houston.

The Polks moved into a boarding-house for married couples. Again, Sarah was happily free of most domestic duties and could devote her days to being a congressman's wife. At first, she was swept into the whirl of receptions, balls, and dinners. Her charming personality and elegant manner

Two States in One

✫ ✫

When the Polks made their journey to Washington in 1826, Virginia was one large state divided by the Blue Ridge Mountains. Virginians east of the mountains and those who lived west were separated by more than terrain, however. Ideas and loyalties also split them apart. The easterners were mostly well-off plantation owners who depended on slave labor. In the west, poorer Virginians lived and worked their own small farms. They resented the power of the planters. In 1861, at the beginning of the Civil War, fifty counties in western Virginia decided to form their own state. They had no wish to support the Confederate cause of their wealthy eastern neighbors. West Virginia was admitted to the Union as the thirty-fifth state in 1863.

Washington as it looked about the time the Polks arrived in 1826

The Capitol as it looked during the years the Polks were in Washington

made her extremely popular at these functions.

James liked socializing far less than Sarah. A few months after Sarah's arrival in Washington, he found it necessary to remind her that they had come to the city to work—and work hard—so he urged her to cut back on party-going. Sarah agreed reluctantly, but used the opportunity to exact a promise from her husband. She wouldn't attend so many functions if he would agree to come to church with her each Sunday. They kept this arrangement for the rest of their lives.

Sarah regularly visited the chambers of the House of Representatives to watch the proceedings.

Sarah began visiting the House chambers regularly. She sat in the ladies' gallery to watch the proceedings. Sarah soon became well versed in currrent policy debates. She frequently surprised James's colleagues with her thorough understanding of the issues.

Sarah also began to take on the role of her husband's private secretary. James had to spend long stretches away from Washington fighting political battles or campaigning in Tennessee. During his absences, Sarah wrote letters, read newspapers, clipped articles and editorials, and sent them to James with her comments. She became, in effect, a key adviser—and James greatly trusted her opinions.

Sarah Polk was sensitive to criticism that her strong political opinions separated her from other Washington wives. Eyebrows were raised, for example, when she stayed with the men in the parlor after a dinner party or when she accompanied James to his office.

But the fact was that James encouraged her interests and preferred that, whenever it was suitable, she be at his side. "He always wished me to go," she wrote, "and he would say, 'Why should you stay at home? To take care of the house? Why, if the house burns down, we can live without it!'" Of course, that's exactly how Sarah felt, too. As usual, they were in complete harmony.

☆   ☆   ☆   ☆   ☆   ☆   ☆   ☆   ☆   ☆   ☆   ☆   ☆   ☆   ☆

CHAPTER FIVE

Home and Back Again

*   *   *   *   *   *   *   *   *   *   *   *   *   *   *

James K. Polk spent fourteen years in Congress. Under the guidance of President Andrew Jackson, he rose through the ranks until he became Speaker of the House in 1835. Because James was Speaker, he and Sarah were at the very top of Washington society. Sarah couldn't have been happier. She counted among her friends interesting, educated women and quite a few influential men.

After fourteen years in Congress, however, James decided not to run again. He would try for the governorship of Tennessee instead. The reasons were complex. Among them was the sense that his presidential

*   *   *   *   *   *   *   *   *   *   *   *   *   *   *

Supreme Court Justice Joseph Story wrote a moving tribute to Sarah when the Polks left Washington after James's last term as a congressman.

charming Sarah Polk, either published in newspapers or read aloud in public. Supreme Court Justice Joseph Story's sweet poem, "To Mrs. Polk on her Leaving Washington," was particularly moving and read in part:

> For I have listened to thy voice,
> And watched thy playful mind,
> Truth in its noblest sense thy
>   choice,
> Yet gentle, graceful, kind.

Back in Tennessee, both Sarah and James jumped into the gubernatorial campaign. Running for office was very different in 1839 than it is today. Rallies were often little more than picnic-type affairs, where candidates would give long-winded speeches. Few of those present followed the speeches closely. There was always a great deal of food and drink and socializing.

James Polk was elected governor in 1839 and served one term. He ran again in 1841 and 1843, but was defeated both times. In a backlash against President Jackson and the Democratic party, Whig party candidates were swept into both national and state offices.

ambitions would be better served as governor than as congressman. His gamble would eventually pay off, but as he and Sarah left Washington for Nashville, she was wistful. There had been many touching tributes to the

James Polk speaking at a political rally during his campaign for governor in 1839

Is There a Speaker in the House?

★ ★ ★ ★ ★ ★ ★ ★ ★ ★ ★ ★ ★ ★ ★ ★ ★ ★ ★

The Speaker of the House has the critical job of keeping the House of Representatives running smoothly. He or she (although there has yet to be a woman Speaker) supervises meetings, maintains order, calls upon those who would like to speak, and appoints committees. The Speaker, who is elected by the party that has the majority in Congress, serves as the head of that party. In the event that both the president and the vice-president are assassinated, the Speaker of the House is next in line for the presidency.

James K. Polk as governor of Tennessee

John Tyler (1790–1862)

✳ ✳

When President William Henry Harrison died a month after his inauguration, Vice-President John Tyler found himself in a new and difficult situation. He was the first vice-president to take over the presidency without being elected to it. A gaunt-looking man with little imagination, he was, in a sense, an "accidental president." The cabinet resigned and the party abandoned him. Even though he had little support, Tyler was determined to be a real president and win the next election. He managed to arrange the annexation of Texas, but without a party behind him, he knew it would be impossible to win an election. As the 1844 presidential race heated up, he withdrew from the running.

For the first time in their seventeen-year marriage, James and Sarah Polk returned to their home in Columbia. James practiced law, managed his family's landholdings, and reacquainted himself with his large extended family. Of course, he kept his eye on the political scene as well.

Eventually, the eyes of the country would be on James again, too. By 1844, President John Tyler was so unpopular that the Whig party did not even renominate him. Henry Clay was chosen instead to face off against the Democratic challenger. But who would that be? Everyone expected that former President Martin Van Buren would be nominated easily. At the Democratic nominating convention, however, the party became dead-

Henry Clay (1777–1852)

★ ★

Henry Clay ran for president five different times and lost each time. Yet, he is remembered as one of the most powerful and influential men in United States history. Although never president, he served in many capacities throughout his political career. As Speaker of the House, he led the "War Hawks" who supported a war with England in 1812. After that, he served as Speaker several more times, as secretary of state, and as a senator. A great legislator, Clay played the role of peacemaker between the North and the South many times in the years before the Civil War.

locked. Finally, after several votes, they chose a most unexpected candidate—former Speaker of the House and former governor of Tennessee, James Knox Polk.

James got the news while lying in a hammock reading the newspaper.

Both he and Sarah were delighted— and not a little surprised—to be back in the political fray. Polk's candidacy surprised many others, too. In fact, the Whigs' favorite campaign slogan became "Who is James Polk?"

Perhaps not surprisingly, Sarah

Everyone expected the Democrats to nominate former President Martin Van Buren (right) as their candidate for president in 1844. Instead, they nominated the relatively unknown James K. Polk.

herself was mentioned in newspaper editorials as a reason either to vote for or—more often—against James Polk. Both her lack of domestic skills and her childlessness were brought up as reasons why she might not make the perfect First Lady. Henry Clay's wife, many would say, kept an immaculate house and churned her own butter. Sarah's reaction was typical of her: "If I get to the White House, I expect to live on $25,000 a year and I will neither keep house nor make butter."

The vote was excruciatingly close,

James Who?

✶ ✶ ✶ ✶ ✶ ✶ ✶ ✶ ✶ ✶ ✶ ✶ ✶ ✶ ✶ ✶ ✶ ✶ ✶ ✶

When Samuel Morse was a young man studying art in London, it took four weeks for news from his family in Massachusetts to reach him. Later in his life, he would change that by inventing the telegraph, a device for communicating instantly by sending electrical impulses through wires. As a message came over the wire in Morse code—a series of taps and pauses that stood for letters—skilled telegraph operators listened to the code and translated it. The first use of this new communication tool by a political party was to send word from Baltimore to Washington of James Polk's Democratic nomination. However, Polk was such a "dark horse," or unlikely winner, that everyone believed the telegraph to be broken.

This torchlight procession in New York City was one of the highlights of Polk's 1844 presidential campaign.

What's a Whig, Anyway?

✯ ✯

Although America has had two political parties since George Washington's time, they have been called by a confusing number of names over the years. At first, Federalists—who supported a strong central government—opposed Anti-Federalists, who wanted the individual states to have more control. By 1800, the Anti-Federalists, led by Thomas Jefferson, were called Democratic Republicans. After 1816, the Federalist party disappeared. The country was left with only one party, which split into two groups. Easterners created the National Republican party. The Democratic party, led by Andrew Jackson, had strong support in the South and West. By 1836, the National Republicans merged with other politicians who disliked Jackson. They formed the Whigs. But the Whigs split over slavery (into "Cotton Whigs" and "Conscience Whigs") and the

Democrats became associated with the proslavery South. Northern Whigs joined Northern Democrats to form the Republican party, which controlled the government for seventy years following the Civil War. With the presidency of Franklin Roosevelt in the 1930s, the Democratic party rose again to power.

A campaign poster for Polk and his running mate, George Mifflin Dallas

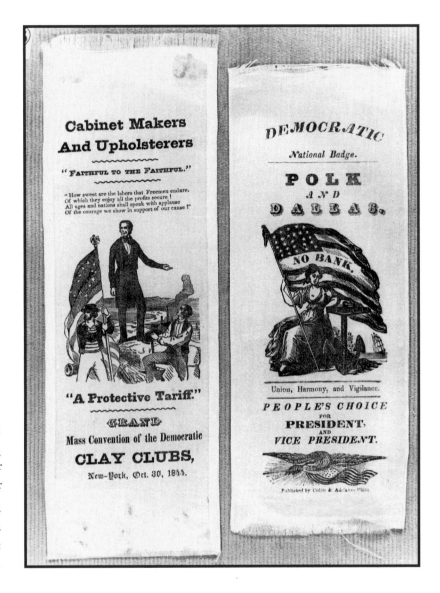

Supporters of the 1844 candidates wore campaign ribbons like these instead of the campaign buttons of today. A Clay Club ribbon is on the left and a ribbon for the Polk-Dallas ticket is on the right.

but when all the ballots were counted, James had won the election by a narrow margin over Henry Clay. Tennesseans were delighted that another of their own would be in the White House. And this time, the state would send a Tennessee-born First Lady, too. (Andrew Jackson had been a widower while he was president.) Now, Sarah Childress Polk would have a chance to leave her mark on history!

CHAPTER SIX

Mr. and Mrs. President

★ ★ ★ ★ ★ ★ ★ ★ ★ ★ ★ ★ ★ ★ ★ ★

The inauguration of the eleventh president of the United States, Mr. James Knox Polk, took place in March 1845 before "a large assemblage of umbrellas," as one reporter noted. It was not yet customary for the president's wife to hold the Bible used to swear her husband into office, or even to ride in the same carriage from the Capitol to the White House. Instead, Sarah Polk was handed a souvenir fan with pictures of the previous First Ladies. She happily accepted this gift—one of the very few she would keep during her husband's presidency—and rode up Pennsylvania Avenue in a carriage with her own friends.

★ ★ ★ ★ ★ ★ ★ ★ ★ ★ ★ ★ ★ ★ ★ ★

Candidate Polk had been very clear about the goals for his presidency. He had four principal objectives, which he promised to accomplish in just four years. Two of his goals involved acquisition of more land for the United States—that is, fulfillment of the doctrine of Manifest Destiny. (The term Manifest Destiny was first used in 1845.) When James Polk took office, the country was bounded on the west and southwest by the Rocky Mountains. He vowed to push the borders to the Rio Grande in the south and the Pacific Ocean in the

Those who attended the inauguration of James K. Polk trudged toward the Capitol in pouring rain (above).

Polk was sworn in as president of the United States in a ceremony held on the steps of the Capitol (right). As one reporter noted, the inauguration took place before "a large assemblage of umbrellas."

After his inauguration, President Polk rode in a carriage up Pennsylvania Avenue to the White House. Sarah rode with friends in a separate carriage.

west. To do this, he would need to negotiate the annexation of Oregon, California, and Texas.

President Polk's two other objectives were domestic in nature. He intended to reduce tariffs and to separate the United States Treasury from the rest of the banking industry. The new president set off on a fatiguing schedule of work and meetings from early in the morning until well past midnight, allowing himself virtually no leisure time. He kept his goals before him and worked diligently.

This nineteenth-century engraving illustrates the doctrine of Manifest Destiny—the belief that the nation was meant to extend across the entire continent, from the Atlantic Ocean to the Pacific Ocean.

The Californios

✯ ✯

About 6,000 people known as *Californios* lived in the Far West at the time of James Polk's presidency. The Californios, of Mexican and Spanish descent, had been born in the area. They were well known for their huge cattle ranches. Indeed, the culture of the Western cowboy truly began with the *vaqueros,* expert horsemen who worked on these ranches. They carried a rope called a *lazo* and wore broad-brimmed hats for protection from the sun and leather *chaperraras* (chaps) over their pants. Once a year, they brought the cattle to market at a roundup called a *rodeo,* a great social event with competitions and parties.

President Polk's cabinet included (standing, left to right) Postmaster General Cave Johnson and Secretary of the Navy George Bancroft; (seated, left to right) Attorney General John Mason, Secretary of War William Marcy, President Polk, and Secretary of the Treasury Robert J. Walker.

Perhaps because of his singlemindedness, he was often thought of as distant and humorless.

The annexion of Texas was actually accomplished just a few days before the Polk Administration began, when President Tyler signed the bill into law. President Polk was so intent on acquiring California, too, that he was fully prepared to go to war with Mexico—in fact, many thought he was willing to provoke a war. When U.S. troops along the Mexican border, under the command of General

This map shows the territorial growth of the United States during the years of expansion.

Zachary Taylor, claimed they were fired on by Mexican forces on April 25, the president requested that a state of war be declared. Congress agreed overwhelmingly. The Mexican War officially began in May 1846.

Not everyone in the United States believed that expansion, much less war to achieve it, was desirable. Antislavery Northerners, an ever-increasing political force, believed President Polk just wanted to expand slavery into new territories. They accused the president of deviousness in his handling of the lands along the Rio Grande and insisted the conflict

The Mexican War: Fast Facts

WHAT: A war to acquire Mexican territory for the United States

WHEN: 1846–1848

WHO: Between the United States and Mexican armies

WHERE: Battles fought as far north as present-day Los Angeles and south to Mexico City

WHY: President James Polk had been unable to purchase California and New Mexico from the Mexican government and decided to take them by force.

OUTCOME: In the Treaty of Guadalupe Hidalgo, Mexico gave the United States the land it wanted, which included southern California and most of the Southwest, in exchange for $15 million. Fifty thousand Mexican soldiers and thirteen thousand Americans died in the conflict.

In a major battle of the Mexican War in May 1846, U.S. troops were victors over Mexican soldiers in Texas.

The Oregon Territory

First mountain men and then missionaries made the great trek and settled in this vast western territory. They sent back stories of land both fertile and free for the taking. Great Britain—which occupied Canada—and the United States agreed that the land, known as Oregon Territory (between the latitudes of 42 degrees north and 54 degrees 40 minutes north), would remain free and open. Expansionist Americans, including Polk, wanted to annex all of the territory and took up the slogan "54-40 or Fight" to express that wish. But war with Mexico was looming, so compromise seemed wise and the United States and Britain negotiated a border at the 49th parallel, which cut through the middle of the Oregon Territory.

Soon after Mexico City was occupied by United States Major General Winfield Scott and his troops (above), the Mexican War ended.

was "Mr. Polk's War." The animosity between North and South that was inflamed by the Mexican War surely helped push the nation toward the Civil War.

Sarah Polk knew that feelings about her husband's policies were strong. Whenever possible, she tried to use her own personal charm to soften the president's image. She insisted he appear with her at the evening public receptions, often having to coax him out of his office to greet the guests. Weekly, she invited thirty or forty important policymakers to dinner at the White House so that issues could be discussed in a cordial setting. She took her duties as White House hostess very seriously. For her, they were not just an end in themselves,

First Lady Sarah Polk (center, next to the president) often invited former First Lady Dolley Madison (second from right) to the White House, and the two became fast friends.

but also a way of furthering the president's political goals.

As First Lady, Sarah generally received favorable notices in the press. For example, she was much praised for inviting beloved former First Lady Dolley Madison to the White House and treating her with tremendous respect. The two strong women became great friends.

Sarah Polk's popularity was all the more remarkable since her strict

Presbyterianism caused her to shun much of the merriment Washington loved. She wouldn't go to the theater or to horse races, both very fashionable at the time. She made sure no music was played within her hearing on Sundays. She forbade dancing at the White House, since she didn't believe it showed proper respect for the great mansion.

Not surprisingly, many people found such rules too harsh. Criticism resurfaced that Sarah controlled everyone—including the president—a little too tightly. Yet such comments, which Sarah had become quite used to over the years, seemed to miss the mark. She was both gracious and feminine, and her deep religious convictions seemed only to add to her integrity.

Sarah would often say to critics that one reason she kept a close eye on her husband's schedule was to protect his health, which had never been good. As his term ended, it was clear the presidency had indeed exhausted Mr. Polk. Sarah was relieved that he would not run for reelection and that they would shortly return to Tennessee.

As promised, all four of President Polk's goals had been achieved within four years. He had used his skills at working with Congress to see banking changes and lowered tariffs become law. The treaty signed at the end of the Mexican War, early in 1848, ceded California and New Mexico to the United States. It also settled the Texas question. The British had reached a compromise with the United States concerning the Oregon Territory earlier in the Polk Administration.

In 1847, Sarah and James bought a lovely home in Nashville, which became known as "Polk Place." Sarah spent several weeks that summer furnishing it, in anticipation of their retirement within a year. Despite her happy years as First Lady, she began to long for the peace and healthfulness retirement would bring.

70

James and Sarah bought Polk Place, a lovely home in Nashville, Tennessee, to be their retirement home after James's term as president was over.

James Polk was frail and exhausted as he and Sarah prepared to leave Washington for the last time. A few days before President-elect Zachary Taylor's inauguration, James wrote, "I am heartily rejoiced that my term is so near its close. I will soon cease to be a servant and will become a sovereign. As a private citizen, I will have no one but myself to serve. . . . I am sure I will be happier in this condition than in the exalted one I now hold."

Zachary Taylor's inauguration ceremony took place on March 5, 1849. The Polks left immediately afterward on their journey to Nashville.

The Polks left the White House and set off immediately on the journey to Nashville, which was to be a grand presidential farewell. Celebrations were planned all along the long southern route, which included stops in Alabama, Mississippi, and Louisiana. The trip would have taxed anyone's stamina, and James Polk was not at all a well man when he left Washington. By the time the Polks arrived in New Orleans, which had had a cholera outbreak, he was extremely weakened.

James never recovered his health sufficiently, even after the couple arrived at Polk Place. He died on June 15, 1849, only three months after leaving office.

James Polk died on June 15, 1849, only three months after leaving office.

CHAPTER SEVEN

A Great Lady

☆ ☆ ☆ ☆ ☆ ☆ ☆ ☆ ☆ ☆ ☆ ☆ ☆ ☆ ☆ ☆

Sarah Polk lived on at Polk Place for forty-two more years. The first years after James's death were difficult ones, although she struggled not to dwell on her loss. To outsiders, it seemed as if she retreated completely from the world, dressing in black, and never leaving Polk Place. When visitors came to call, she took them into James's study, where everything was exactly as he'd left it in 1849.

Sarah's life, however, gradually became full and happy, if not as eventful as it had once been. She received many visitors each day, among them an extended family of the very young and the very old.

☆ ☆ ☆ ☆ ☆ ☆ ☆ ☆ ☆ ☆ ☆ ☆ ☆ ☆ ☆ ☆

Sarah Polk's orphaned grandniece, Sarah Polk Jetton (left), went to live with Sarah at Polk Place soon after James Polk's death.

After James's death, Sarah Polk dressed in black and wore a widow's cap.

An orphaned grand-niece, Sarah Polk Jetton, came to live with her as a daughter.

When Sarah Jetton was grown, she and her family returned to live with Grandaunt Sarah. Polk Place, in fact, was often bursting with the sounds of children.

Sarah also received guests from around Tennessee and the nation. She treated the eminent and the unassuming with equal courtesy. The Tennessee General Assembly paid her a visit each New Year's Day. Any parade in Nashville included Polk Place on its route, as a kind of unofficial reviewing stand. The marchers would pause long enough for Sarah, dressed in black and wearing a widow's cap, to come to the window and wave.

Tough Tennesseans

★ ★

As a port and railroad hub, Nashville, Tennessee, was an important conquest and base for Union forces during the Civil War. General John Hood's Confederate Army of Tennessee tried desperately to force Union troops out of the state in the Battle of Nashville on December 15 and 16, 1864. Tennesseans had a reputation as tough fighting men, but the Union army defeated them at Nashville once and for all. Throughout the Civil War, more bloody battles were fought in Tennessee than in any other state except Virginia.

William Tecumseh Sherman (1820–1891)

✷ ✷

This intense and fierce-looking Union general fought in many of the major Civil War battles. Toward the end of the war, Sherman moved his forces from Chattanooga, Tennessee, to capture Atlanta, Georgia, the last important railroad center of the Confederacy. When Confederate forces cut off his supply line from the north, he marched his men 300 miles (483 km) to the sea, where the Union navy had supplies. He ordered his men to eat off the land as they marched, taking whatever they found. To discourage the Confederates from following and engaging his army when they were unable to fight, he ordered his men to destroy anything they did not use. Sherman's army left a path of destruction 60 miles (97 km) wide and 300 miles (483 km) long during its infamous "march to the sea."

The Civil War (1861–1865) was difficult for everyone in Nashville. The Polk and Childress families were firm Confederates, but Sarah was convinced that President Polk would have opposed secession. She insisted, therefore, that Polk Place be considered neutral ground. Astonishingly, both Northern and Southern generals honored her wishes. When William Tecumseh Sherman, the hated Union army general, paid Sarah a call, she greeted even him with polite, if formal, courtesy.

79

Profile of America, 1891: Promises Made and Broken

✫ ✫

Sarah Polk's life spanned almost an exact century, from 1803 to 1891. She lived through a civil war and an industrial revolution. By the time of Sarah's death, America was a very different place than it had been in 1803. It included 44 states and 64 million people.

Even though most Americans still worked on farms in 1891, industry set the country's fast pace. Factories poured out goods from furniture to food; few things were still made by hand. Cities grew tall with new skyscrapers, and they bustled with country folk and thousands of European immigrants seeking jobs and good fortune. Women flooded into the big cities where they might find work as book-keepers or office clerks. But the promise was often hollow, especially for the Europeans. Work was hard and hours were long, tenements were crowded and the air was choked with factory smoke.

Nearly all of these Sioux Indians, assembled for a dance at Wounded Knee in August 1890, were killed by U.S. troops only a few months later, on December 29.

If 1891 held the promise of prosperity for some Americans, it marked the ending of ancient Native American ways. On January 16, 1891, the Sioux surrendered at Wounded Knee, just weeks after U.S. troops had fired into the encampment killing 200 men, women, and children. It was the last straw for the struggling Indian people. The buffalo were gone, and hunting grounds had been taken over. Jefferson's 1803 pledge to be "neighborly, friendly, and useful" to the Indians had long been broken. Instead, Black Elk, an Oglala Sioux, believed that, by 1891, "a people's dream died."

Far from such sadness, in cities and suburbs, many Americans by 1891 had more time for leisure. Everyone rode bicycles for fun. Men, women, and children took to the roads, and bicycle clubs thrived. Cycling ladies wore their skirts scandalously short—just above

James Naismith, shown here with his wife, invented the game of basketball at the Springfield, Massachusetts, YMCA in 1891, the year of Sarah Polk's death.

the ankle—to make pedaling easier. Thomas Edison patented his "kinetoscopic camera" in 1891, a new-fangled device that took moving pictures on a strip of film. Another invention, the zipper, revolutionized the fashion industry. At the YMCA in Springfield, Massachusetts, James Naismith attached peach baskets to the walls and organized teams to throw balls into them. African-American jockey Isaac Murphy became the first three-time winner of the Kentucky Derby.

James and Sarah Polk are buried together in this tomb on the grounds of the capitol in Nashville, Tennessee.

The war left Sarah Polk in financial need. In 1860, she'd sold her Mississippi plantation, her main source of income, for $30,000. There was, as yet, no federal pension given to the surviving wives of former presidents, although many had sought one for Dolley Madison, who had lived in near-poverty at the end of her life. In 1882, Congress finally awarded Sarah Polk an annual pension of $5,000.

Sarah Childress Polk died quietly at Polk Place on August 14, 1891, just a few weeks before her eighty-eighth birthday. She was buried in the garden, beside her beloved James. In a dignified procession in 1892, the remains of President Polk and First Lady Sarah Polk were reinterred on the grounds of the capitol building in Nashville, Tennessee, where they are today.

The Presidents and Their First Ladies

| YEARS IN OFFICE | | | |
President	Birth–Death	First Lady	Birth–Death
1789–1797			
George Washington	1732–1799	Martha Dandridge Custis Washington	1731–1802
1797–1801			
John Adams	1735–1826	Abigail Smith Adams	1744–1818
1801–1809			
Thomas Jefferson†	1743–1826		
1809–1817			
James Madison	1751–1836	Dolley Payne Todd Madison	1768–1849
1817–1825			
James Monroe	1758–1831	Elizabeth Kortright Monroe	1768–1830
1825–1829			
John Quincy Adams	1767–1848	Louisa Catherine Johnson Adams	1775–1852
1829–1837			
Andrew Jackson†	1767–1845	Rachel Donelson Jackson	1767–1828
1837–1841			
Martin Van Buren†	1782–1862		
1841			
William Henry Harrison‡	1773–1841		
1841–1845			
John Tyler	1790–1862	Letitia Christian Tyler (1841–1842)	1790–1842
		Julia Gardiner Tyler (1844–1845)	1820–1889
1845–1849			
James K. Polk	1795–1849	Sarah Childress Polk	1803–1891
1849–1850			
Zachary Taylor	1784–1850	Margaret Mackall Smith Taylor	1788–1852
1850–1853			
Millard Fillmore	1800–1874	Abigail Powers Fillmore	1798–1853
1853–1857			
Franklin Pierce	1804–1869	Jane Means Appleton Pierce	1806–1863
1857–1861			
James Buchanan*	1791–1868		
1861–1865			
Abraham Lincoln	1809–1865	Mary Todd Lincoln	1818–1882
1865–1869			
Andrew Johnson	1808–1875	Eliza McCardle Johnson	1810–1876
1869–1877			
Ulysses S. Grant	1822–1885	Julia Dent Grant	1826–1902
1877–1881			
Rutherford B. Hayes	1822–1893	Lucy Ware Webb Hayes	1831–1889
1881			
James A. Garfield	1831–1881	Lucretia Rudolph Garfield	1832–1918
1881–1885			
Chester A. Arthur†	1829–1886		

† wife died before he took office   ‡ wife too ill to accompany him to Washington   * never married

1885–1889			
Grover Cleveland	1837–1908	Frances Folsom Cleveland	1864–1947
1889–1893			
Benjamin Harrison	1833–1901	Caroline Lavinia Scott Harrison	1832–1892
1893–1897			
Grover Cleveland	1837–1908	Frances Folsom Cleveland	1864–1947
1897–1901			
William McKinley	1843–1901	Ida Saxton McKinley	1847–1907
1901–1909			
Theodore Roosevelt	1858–1919	Edith Kermit Carow Roosevelt	1861–1948
1909–1913			
William Howard Taft	1857–1930	Helen Herron Taft	1861–1943
1913–1921			
Woodrow Wilson	1856–1924	Ellen Louise Axson Wilson (1913–1914)	1860–1914
		Edith Bolling Galt Wilson (1915–1921)	1872–1961
1921–1923			
Warren G. Harding	1865–1923	Florence Kling Harding	1860–1924
1923–1929			
Calvin Coolidge	1872–1933	Grace Anna Goodhue Coolidge	1879–1957
1929–1933			
Herbert Hoover	1874–1964	Lou Henry Hoover	1874–1944
1933–1945			
Franklin D. Roosevelt	1882–1945	Anna Eleanor Roosevelt	1884–1962
1945–1953			
Harry S. Truman	1884–1972	Bess Wallace Truman	1885–1982
1953–1961			
Dwight D. Eisenhower	1890–1969	Mamie Geneva Doud Eisenhower	1896–1979
1961–1963			
John F. Kennedy	1917–1963	Jacqueline Bouvier Kennedy	1929–1994
1963–1969			
Lyndon B. Johnson	1908–1973	Claudia Taylor (Lady Bird) Johnson	1912–
1969–1974			
Richard Nixon	1913–1994	Patricia Ryan Nixon	1912–1993
1974–1977			
Gerald Ford	1913–	Elizabeth Bloomer Ford	1918–
1977–1981			
James Carter	1924–	Rosalynn Smith Carter	1927–
1981–1989			
Ronald Reagan	1911–	Nancy Davis Reagan	1923–
1989–1993			
George Bush	1924–	Barbara Pierce Bush	1925–
1993–			
William Jefferson Clinton	1946–	Hillary Rodham Clinton	1947–

Sarah Childress Polk
Timeline

1793 ★ James K. Polk is born
Louis XVI and Marie Antoinette are executed in Paris
Eli Whitney invents the cotton gin

1794 ★ Thomas Paine writes *The Age of Reason*

1795 ★ Eleventh Amendment is added to the U.S.
Constitution

1796 ★ Tennessee becomes a state
George Washington gives his Farewell Address
John Adams is elected president

1798 ★ Eli Whitney introduces interchangeable parts

1800 ★ U.S. population is 5,308,483
Federal government moves to Washington, D.C.
Thomas Jefferson is elected president
France regains the Louisiana Territory from Spain
Library of Congress is founded

1801 ★ Robert Fulton invents the submarine

1802 ★ U.S. Military Academy opens at West Point, New York

1803 ★ United States purchases Louisiana Territory from
France
Sarah Childress is born on September 4
Ohio becomes a state
Robert Fulton invents the steamboat

1804 ★ Lewis and Clark expedition begins
Thomas Jefferson is reelected president

1805 ★ Twelfth Amendment is added to the U.S. Constitution
United States wins a major victory against the Barbary
Coast pirates

1808	★	James Madison is elected president
1809	★	Washington Irving writes *Rip Van Winkle*
1810	★	U.S. population is 7,239,881
1811	★	James Madison restricts trade with Great Britain
1812	★	United States declares war on Great Britain
		James Madison is reelected president
		Louisiana becomes a state
1813	★	During War of 1812, U.S. Army captures Toronto, Canada, and U.S Navy defeats British on Lake Erie
		Mexico declares its independence from Spain
1814	★	British burn Washington, D.C.
		Francis Scott Key writes "The Star-Spangled Banner"
		Treaty of Ghent officially ends the War of 1812
1815	★	Andrew Jackson defeats the British at the Battle of New Orleans after the War of 1812 officially ended
1816	★	James Monroe is elected president
		Indiana becomes a state
1817	★	Mississippi becomes a state
1818	★	United States and Great Britain agree on a permanent border between the United States and part of Canada at the 49th parallel
		Illinois becomes a state
1819	★	Alabama becomes a state
1820	★	U.S. population is 9,638,453
		James Monroe is reelected president
		Missouri Compromise admits Maine as a free state and Missouri as a slave state
1821	★	First Americans settle in Mexican-controlled territory of Texas
		Mexico wins independence from Spain

1823	★	Monroe Doctrine proclaims the Americas off-limits to European powers
		Mexico becomes a republic
1824	★	Sarah Childress marries James K. Polk
		John Quincy Adams is elected president after a disputed election
1825	★	Erie Canal opens, connecting New York City to cities on the Great Lakes
1826	★	James Fenimore Cooper's *The Last of the Mohicans* is published
		John Adams and Thomas Jefferson die on July 4
1828	★	Andrew Jackson is elected president
		Noah Webster's *The American Dictionary of the English Language* is published
1829	★	*Encyclopedia Americana*, the first U.S. encyclopedia, is published
		Englishman James Smithson leaves money to found the Smithsonian Institution
1830	★	U.S. population is 12,866,020
		Joseph Smith founds the Mormon church
1831	★	William Lloyd Garrison publishes *The Liberator*, an antislavery newspaper
1832	★	Andrew Jackson is reelected president
		New England Anti-Slavery Society is founded in Boston
1833	★	Whig party is established
		Oberlin College becomes the first college to admit women
		Slavery is abolished throughout the British Empire
1835	★	Samuel Morse builds the first telegraph
		Texas declares its right to secede from Mexico
1836	★	Martin Van Buren is elected president
		Texas declares independence from Mexico
		Texans are defeated at the Alamo

1837	★	Economic depression spreads throughout the United States
		Michigan becomes a state
1840	★	U.S. population is 17,069,453
		William Henry Harrison is elected president
1841	★	William Henry Harrison dies a month after taking office and John Tyler becomes president
1842	★	Massachusetts Supreme Court recognizes labor unions
		Massachusetts passes laws regulating child labor
1844	★	James K. Polk is elected president
1845	★	Texas and Florida become states
		U.S. Naval Academy opens at Annapolis, Maryland
1846	★	United States declares war on Mexico
		United States annexes New Mexico from Mexico
		John Deere constructs a steel plow
		Oregon Territory is divided between the United States and Great Britain at the 49th parallel

1847	★	U.S. Army captures Mexico City
		Maria Mitchell is the first woman elected to the American Academy of Arts and Sciences
		Smithsonian Institution is formally dedicated
1848	★	Treaty of Guadalupe Hidalgo ends the Mexican War and gives most of the present-day Southwest to the United States
		First U.S. women's rights meeting is held in Seneca Falls, New York
		Gold is discovered in California
		First medical school for women is opened in Boston, Massachusetts
		Zachary Taylor is elected president
		Wisconsin becomes a state
1849	★	James K. Polk dies
		Elizabeth Blackwell becomes the first woman in the world to receive a medical degree
		California gold rush starts

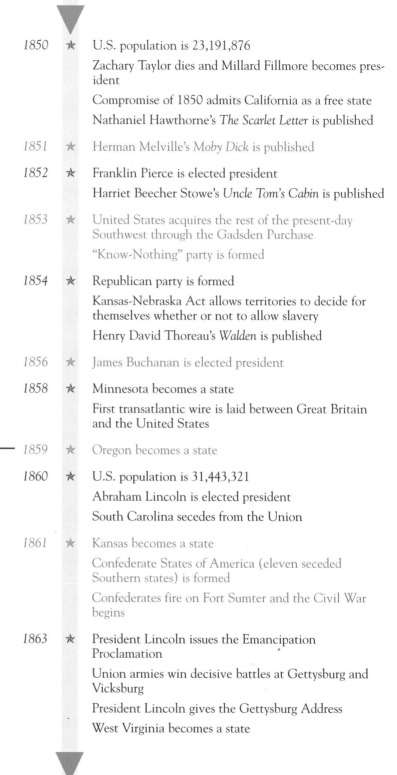

1850 ★ U.S. population is 23,191,876

Zachary Taylor dies and Millard Fillmore becomes president

Compromise of 1850 admits California as a free state

Nathaniel Hawthorne's *The Scarlet Letter* is published

1851 ★ Herman Melville's *Moby Dick* is published

1852 ★ Franklin Pierce is elected president

Harriet Beecher Stowe's *Uncle Tom's Cabin* is published

1853 ★ United States acquires the rest of the present-day Southwest through the Gadsden Purchase

"Know-Nothing" party is formed

1854 ★ Republican party is formed

Kansas-Nebraska Act allows territories to decide for themselves whether or not to allow slavery

Henry David Thoreau's *Walden* is published

1856 ★ James Buchanan is elected president

1858 ★ Minnesota becomes a state

First transatlantic wire is laid between Great Britain and the United States

1859 ★ Oregon becomes a state

1860 ★ U.S. population is 31,443,321

Abraham Lincoln is elected president

South Carolina secedes from the Union

1861 ★ Kansas becomes a state

Confederate States of America (eleven seceded Southern states) is formed

Confederates fire on Fort Sumter and the Civil War begins

1863 ★ President Lincoln issues the Emancipation Proclamation

Union armies win decisive battles at Gettysburg and Vicksburg

President Lincoln gives the Gettysburg Address

West Virginia becomes a state

1864	★	Union army invades Virginia for the final campaign of the war
		General Sherman captures Atlanta
		Abraham Lincoln is reelected president
		Nevada becomes a state
1865	★	Civil War ends when Robert E. Lee surrenders the Confederate army to Union general Ulysses S. Grant
		Abraham Lincoln is assassinated
		Andrew Johnson becomes president
		Thirteenth Amendment is added to the U.S. Constitution, which ends slavery
1866	★	Transatlantic cable between Great Britain and the United States is completed
1867	★	United States purchases Alaska from Russia
		Labor unions win the right to an eight-hour day in Illinois, New York, and Missouri
1868	★	President Andrew Johnson is impeached by the U.S. House of Representatives but is acquitted by the U.S. Senate
		Fourteenth Amendment is added to the Constitution Ulysses S. Grant is elected president
		Louisa May Alcott's *Little Women* is published
1869	★	First U.S. transcontinental railroad is completed
		Wyoming Territory allows women to vote
		National Women Suffrage Association is founded
		The first professional baseball team, the Cincinnati Red Stockings, is formed
1870	★	U.S. population is 39,818,449
		Fifteenth Amendment is added to the U. S. Constitution
		First African American takes a seat in Congress
1871	★	Great Chicago Fire destroys most of the city
		First professional baseball league is formed
		Barnum's Circus opens in New York City
		National Rifle Association is founded

1872	★	Susan B. Anthony is arrested for trying to vote
		Ulysses S. Grant is reelected president
		Yellowstone National Park, the nation's first, is established
1873	★	Panic of 1873 sets off a five-year depression
		San Francisco installs a cable-car system
1874	★	First public zoo in United States opens in Philadelphia
1875	★	Baseball glove is invented
1876	★	George Armstrong Custer and his troops are killed at the Battle of the Little Bighorn
		Alexander Graham Bell successfully tests the telephone
		Colorado becomes a state
		Mark Twain's *The Adventures of Tom Sawyer* is published
1877	★	Rutherford B. Hayes becomes president
		Thomas Edison patents the phonograph
		U.S. Army captures Chief Joseph of the Nez Perce
		First public telephones appear in the United States
1878	★	First bicycles are manufactured in the United States
		Knights of Labor is founded
1879	★	Women lawyers win the right to argue cases before the Supreme Court
		Frank Woolworth opens his first five-and-ten-cent store
1880	★	U.S. population is 50,155,783
		James Garfield is elected president
		Salvation Army opens in the United States
1881	★	James A. Garfield is shot and dies ninety days later
		Chester A. Arthur becomes president
		American branch of the Red Cross opens
1882	★	Congress approves a pension for all widows of U.S. presidents
		Jesse James, famous Western outlaw, is shot and killed

1883	★	Brooklyn Bridge opens in New York City
		"Buffalo Bill's Wild West Show" begins touring the United States
1884	★	Grover Cleveland is elected president
		Mark Twain's *Huckleberry Finn* is published
1885	★	Washington Monument is dedicated in Washington, D.C.
1886	★	Statue of Liberty, a gift from France, is dedicated
		Geronimo and the Apache surrender to the U.S. Army
		American Federation of Labor is organized
1888	★	Benjamin Harrison is elected president
		George Eastman introduces the Kodak camera
1889	★	Montana, Washington, North Dakota, and South Dakota become states
1890	★	U.S. population is 62,947,714
		Idaho and Wyoming become states
1891	★	Joe Naismith invents basketball
		Sarah Childress Polk dies on August 14

Fast Facts about
Sarah Childress Polk

Born: September 4, 1803, on a plantation near Murfreesboro, Tennessee

Died: August 14, 1891, in Nashville, Tennessee

First Burial Site: Polk Place in Nashville, Tennessee

Permanent Burial Site: State Capitol grounds in Nashville, Tennessee

Parents: Joel Childress and Elizabeth Whitsitt Childress

Education: Public school, Murfreesboro; private instruction at Bradley Academy, Murfreesboro; Mr. Abercrombie's School for Young Ladies, Nashville; Moravian Female Academy, Salem, North Carolina.

Marriage: To James K. Polk on January 1, 1824, until his death in 1849

Children: None

Places She Lived: Plantation near Murfreesboro, Tennessee (1803–1824); Nashville, Tennessee (1824–26, 1839–41, 1849–91); Washington, D.C. (1826–39, 1845–49); Columbia, Tennessee (1841–1845)

Major Achievements:
- ⋆ Served as personal secretary to her husband, President James K. Polk
- ⋆ Became the first First Lady who was brought into the daily workings of her husband's administration
- ⋆ Held weekly dinners at the White House for thirty or forty policymakers so issues could be discussed in a cordial, social setting
- ⋆ Held public receptions at the White House on Tuesday and Friday evenings and insisted that President Polk attend so that he could keep in touch with the people
- ⋆ Added gas lighting to the White House

Fast Facts about
James K. Polk's Presidency

Terms of Office: Elected in 1844; served as the eleventh president of the United States from 1845 to 1849

Vice President: George M. Dallas (1845–1849)

Major Policy Decisions and Legislation:
* Strongly believed in Manifest Destiny and nearly doubled the size of the United States by adding land in the Southwest and Northwest during his administration
* Asked Congress to declare war on Mexico, which led to the Mexican War (1846–1848)
* Signed the Walker Tariff Act (1846) that lowered taxes on imported goods
* Signed the Treasury bill of 1846 that allowed the federal government to be its own banker

Major Events:
* The United States fought and won the Mexican War, resulting in the United States gaining most of the present-day Southwest.
* The United States and Great Britain agreed on the 49th parallel as their boundary in the Oregon Territory.
* Texas (1845), Iowa (1846), and Wisconsin (1848) were admitted as states.
* Levi Woodbury (1845) and Robert C. Grier (1846) were appointed associate justices of the United States Supreme Court by James K. Polk.

Where to Visit

The Capitol Building
Constitution Avenue
Washington, D.C.
(202) 225-3121

Lewis and Clark Trail Heritage Foundation (LCTHF)
Box 3434
Great Falls, Montana 59403
(406) 453-7091

Moravian Historical Society
214 E. Center Street
Nazareth, Pennsylvania 18064
(610) 759-5070

National Archives
Constitution Avenue
Washington, D.C.
(202) 501-5000

"Polk Place"
University of North Carolina at Chapel Hill, South Campus
Chapel Hill, North Carolina
(919) 962-1630

The White House
1600 Pennsylvania Avenue
Washington, D.C
(202) 456-7041

White House Historical Association (WHHA)
740 Jackson Place NW
Washington, D.C. 20503
(202) 737-8292

Online Sites of Interest

The First Ladies of the United States of America

http://www2.whitehouse.gov/WH/glimpse/firstladies/html/firstladies.html

A portrait and biographical sketch of each First Lady plus links to White House sites

Grolier Online

http://www.grolier.com/presidents/aae/inaugs/1845polk.html

This site includes a biography, the full text of Polk's inaugural address, and quick facts about President James K. Polk.

University of North Carolina at Chapel Hill

http://www.adp.unc.edu/sis/admissions/grad/ctour09a.html

This section of the University of North Carolina at Chapel Hill's website gives a tour of "Polk Place," the area of the university's campus that James K. Polk's dorm room overlooked. Also includes a short biography of Polk.

University of San Diego

http://ac.acusd.edu/History/classes/diplo/mexwar.html

Provides facts about Polk's involvement with the Mexican War, a chronology of the war, and the complete text of the Treaty of Guadalupe Hidalgo, which ended the war in 1848.

The White House

http://www.whitehouse.gov/WH/Welcome.html

Information about the current president and vice president; White House history; biographies of past presidents and their families; a virtual tour of the White House; current events taking place at the White House, and much more.

The White House for Kids

http://www.whitehouse.gov/WH/kids/html/kidshome.html

Includes information about White House kids, past and present; famous "First Pets," past and present; historic moments of the presidency; and much more.

For Further Reading

Carter, Alden R. *The Mexican War: Manifest Destiny*. New York: Franklin Watts, 1992.

Gould, Lewis L. (ed). *American First Ladies: Their Lives and Their Legacy*. New York: Garland Publishing, 1996.

Klapthor, Margaret Brown. *The First Ladies*. Washington, D.C.: White House Historical Association in cooperation with the National Geographic Society, 1994.

Lillegard, Dee. *James K. Polk: Eleventh President of the United States*. Chicago: Childrens Press, 1988.

Lindsey, Rae. *The Presidents' First Ladies*. New York: Franklin Watts, 1989.

Mayo, Edith P. (ed.). *The Smithsonian Book of the First Ladies: Their Lives, Times, and Issues*. New York: Henry Holt, 1996.

Nardo, Don. *The Mexican-American War*. San Diego: Lucent Books, 1991.

Index

Page numbers in **boldface type** indicate illustrations

N

Naismith, James, 81, **81**
Nashville, Tennessee, 19, 48
  burial of Polks at capitol
    building in, **82**, 83
  in Civil War, 78, 79
  governor's office in, 25
  Polk Place in, **71**, 75, 77,
    79
  as a port and railroad hub,
    78
  presidential farewell route
    to, 72
National Park, Great Smoky
  Mountains, 22
National Republican party,
  55
National Road, 37, **37**
Native Americans
  changes for, 81
  Cherokee people as, 22
  government policy toward,
    30
  Jefferson's promises to, 81
  and Lewis and Clark expe-
    dition, 17
  Sioux Indians as, **80**, 81
  and Wounded Knee, **80**,
    81
New Mexico, acquisition of,
  70
New Orleans
  cholera outbreak in, 72
  presidential farewell route
    through, 72
North Carolina, claim of
  lands of Tennessee by,
  33

O

Oglala Sioux, 81
Ohio, statehood for, 17
Ohio Valley, settlement of,
  17
Old Hickory, 27
online sites of interest, 97
Oregon, annexation of, 61
Oregon Territory, 66, **66**, 70,
  90, 95

P

Pacific Islands, U.S. acquisition of, 13
Pacific Ocean, 60
Pennsylvania Avenue, 59,
  61
plank roads, 37
Political parties. *See* Anti-
  Federalists; Democratic
  party; Democratic-Re-
  publicans; Federalists;
  National Republican
  party; Republican party;
  Whig party
Polk, James K.
  absences from home, 36,
    39, 44
  admission to Tennessee
    bar, 27
  belief in Manifest Destiny,
    11, 13, 60–61, 95
  cabinet of, **63**
  campaign style of, **28**,
    29
  as candidate for Tennessee
    House of Repre-
    sentatives, 29

as candidate for Ten-
  nessee's congressional
  seat, 36
career as congressman, 47
church-going habits of,
  28–29, 43
courtship of Sarah by, 27–
  28
Dallas as running mate, **56**,
  95
death of, 72
decision not to run for
  reelection as president,
  70
decision to run for governor of Tennessee, 47–48
and 1844 Democratic nom-
  inating convention, 51–
  52, 54
dislike of socializing, 43
election as chief clerk of
  state senate, 26, **26**,
  27
election as congressman,
  36
election as governor in
  1839, **49**
in election of 1844, 52–53,
  54, **56**, 57, **57**
facts about, 95
friendship with Anderson
  Childress, 18–19, 26
friendship with Andrew
  Jackson, 27, 28, 35–36
goals of, as president, 60,
  61, 68, 70
as governor of Tennessee,
  48, **50**, 52

Photo Identifications

Cover: First Lady Sarah Childress Polk
Page 8:   Sarah and James K. Polk about 1848
Page 14:   Stone's River, near Murfreesboro, Tennessee
Page 24:   Murfreesboro, Tennessee, 1893 about a block from the town square
Page 34:   Sara and James, 1826
Page 46:   A hand-colored lithograph of Sarah Polk by Nathaniel Currier
Page 58:   Presidential portrait of James K. Polk by George P. A. Healy
Page 74:   A portrait of Sarah Polk painted about 1849–1850

Photo Credits©

About the Author

Susan Sinnott began her publishing career as an editor for *Cricket*, a literary magazine for children. She later worked for the University of Wisconsin Press, where she managed and edited academic journals. Eventually, her own children pulled her away from scholarly publishing, and helped her rediscover the joys of reading and writing books for young people. Ms. Sinnott's books include *Extraordinary Hispanic Americans* and *Extraordinary Asian Pacific Americans* (for Children's Press) and *Chinese Railroad Workers* and *Doing Our Part: American Women on the Home Front During World War II* (Franklin Watts).